What Is Found There:
Notebooks on Poetry and Politics

Collected Early Poems
1950–1970

An Atlas of the Difficult World:
Poems 1988–1991

Time's Power: Poems 1985–1988

Blood, Bread, and Poetry: Selected Prose 1979–1986

Your Native Land, Your Life

The Fact of a Doorframe: Poems Selected and New 1950–1984

Sources

A Wild Patience Has Taken Me This Far

On Lies, Secrets, and Silence: Selected Prose, 1966–1978

The Dream of a Common Language

Twenty-one Love Poems

Of Woman Born: Motherhood As Experience and Institution

Poems: Selected and New, 1950–1974

Diving into the Wreck

The Will to Change

Leaflets

Necessities of Life

Snapshots of a Daughter-in-Law

The Diamond Cutters

A Change of World

DARK FIELDS
OF THE
REPUBLIC

DARK FIELDS
OF THE
REPUBLIC

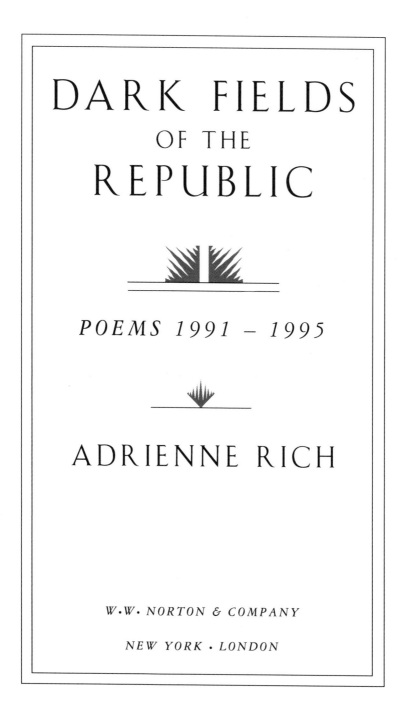

POEMS 1991 – 1995

ADRIENNE RICH

W·W· NORTON & COMPANY

NEW YORK · LONDON

Excerpt from "The World Is Falling Down," composed and sung by Abbey Lincoln, from her album *The World Is Falling Down*. Reprinted by permission of Abbey Lincoln.

Excerpt from "Canzone" from *W. H. Auden: Collected Poems* by W. H. Auden, edited by Edward Mendelson. Copyright © 1943 by W. H. Auden. Copyright renewed 1971 by W. H. Auden. Reprinted by permission of Random House, Inc. and Faber and Faber Ltd.

Excerpt from Medbh McGuckian's postcard reprinted with permission.

Excerpt from *The Letters of Rosa Luxemburg*, edited, translated and with an introduction by Stephen Eric Bronner, published by Humanities Press International, Inc., Atlantic Highlands, N.J. Reprinted with permission.

I thank the Academy of American Poets and the John D. and Catherine T. MacArthur Foundation for generous support at critical times.

My thanks also to the periodicals where many of these poems first appeared, sometimes in earlier versions: *Agni, American Poetry Review, Bombay Gin, Cream City Review, Field, Long Shot, Many Mountains Moving Review, Paris Review, Poetry Ireland Review, Princeton Library Chronicle, Sifrut, Southwest Review, The Village Voice, The Yale Review.*

The text of this book is composed in 11 on 13 Garamond #3
with the display set in Bauer Text initials.
Composition by PennSet, Inc.
Manufacturing by Courier Companies, Inc.
Book design by Antonina Krass

Library of Congress Cataloging-in-Publication Data
Rich, Adrienne Cecile.
Dark Fields of the Republic: Poems 1991–1995 / Adrienne Rich.
p.   cm.
I. Title.
PS3535.I233D37   1995
811'.54—dc20   95-2272
ISBN 0-393-03868-8
ISBN 0-393-31398-0 (pbk.)

W. W. Norton & Company, Inc., 500 Fifth Avenue, New York, NY 10110
W. W. Norton & Company Ltd., 10 Coptic Street, London WC1A 1PU

1   2   3   4   5   6   7   8   9   0

CONTENTS

He had come a long way to this blue lawn, and his dream must have seemed so close that he could hardly fail to grasp it. He did not know that it was already behind him, somewhere back in that vast obscurity beyond the city, where the dark fields of the republic rolled on under the night.

—*The Great Gatsby*

WHAT KIND OF
TIMES ARE THESE

WHAT KIND OF TIMES ARE THESE

There's a place between two stands of trees where the grass grows
        uphill
and the old revolutionary road breaks off into shadows
near a meeting-house abandoned by the persecuted
who disappeared into those shadows.

I've walked there picking mushrooms at the edge of dread, but
        don't be fooled,
this isn't a Russian poem, this is not somewhere else but here,
our country moving closer to its own truth and dread,
its own ways of making people disappear.

I won't tell you where the place is, the dark mesh of the woods
meeting the unmarked strip of light—
ghost-ridden crossroads, leafmold paradise:
I know already who wants to buy it, sell it, make it disappear.

And I won't tell you where it is, so why do I tell you
anything? Because you still listen, because in times like these
to have you listen at all, it's necessary
to talk about trees.

1991

IN THOSE YEARS

In those years, people will say, we lost track
of the meaning of *we*, of *you*
we found ourselves
reduced to *I*
and the whole thing became
silly, ironic, terrible:
we were trying to live a personal life
and, yes, that was the only life
we could bear witness to

But the great dark birds of history screamed and plunged
into our personal weather
They were headed somewhere else but their beaks and pinions drove
along the shore, through the rags of fog
where we stood, saying *I*

1991

TO THE DAYS

From you I want more than I've ever asked,
all of it—the newscasts' terrible stories
of life in my time, the knowing it's worse than that,
much worse—the knowing what it means to be lied to.

Fog in the mornings, hunger for clarity,
coffee and bread with sour plum jam.
Numbness of soul in placid neighborhoods.
Lives ticking on as if.

A typewriter's torrent, suddenly still.
Blue soaking through fog, two dragonflies wheeling.
Acceptable levels of cruelty, steadily rising.
Whatever you bring in your hands, I need to see it.

Suddenly I understand the verb without tenses.
To smell another woman's hair, to taste her skin.
To know the bodies drifting underwater.
To be human, said Rosa—I can't teach you that.

A cat drinks from a bowl of marigolds—his moment.
Surely the love of life is never-ending,
the failure of nerve, a charred fuse?
I want more from you than I ever knew to ask.

Wild pink lilies erupting, tasseled stalks of corn
in the Mexican gardens, corn and roses.
Shortening days, strawberry fields in ferment
with tossed-aside, bruised fruit.

1991

MIRACLE ICE CREAM

MIRACLE's truck comes down the little avenue,
Scott Joplin ragtime strewn behind it like pearls,
and, yes, you can feel happy
with one piece of your heart.

Take what's still given: in a room's rich shadow
a woman's breasts swinging lightly as she bends
Early now the pearl of dusk dissolves.
Late, you sit weighing the evening news,
fast-food miracles, ghostly revolutions,
the rest of your heart.

1992

RACHEL

There's a girl born in abrupt August light
far north, a light soon to be peeled
like an onion, down to nothing. Around her ions are falling
in torrents, glacial eyes are staring, the monster's body
trapped in the bay goes through its spasms.
What she opens her gray eyes on
is drastic. Even the man and woman gazing
into her unfocused gaze, searching for focus,
are drastic.
     It's the end of a century.
If she gets to grow old, if there's anything
: anyone to speak, will they say of her,
She grew up to see it, she was our mother, but
she was born one of them?

1992

AMENDS

Nights like this: on the cold apple-bough
a white star, then another
exploding out of the bark:
on the ground, moonlight picking at small stones

as it picks at greater stones, as it rises with the surf
laying its cheek for moments on the sand
as it licks the broken ledge, as it flows up the cliffs,
as it flicks across the tracks

as it unavailing pours into the gash
of the sand-and-gravel quarry
as it leans across the hangared fuselage
of the crop-dusting plane

as it soaks through cracks into the trailers
tremulous with sleep
as it dwells upon the eyelids of the sleepers
as if to make amends

1992

CALLE VISIÓN

1

Not what you thought: just a turn-off
leading downhill not up

narrow, doesn't waste itself
has a house at the far end

scrub oak and cactus in the yard
some cats   some snakes

in the house there is a room
in the room there is a bed

on the bed there is a blanket
that tells the coming of the railroad

under the blanket there are sheets
scrubbed transparent here and there

under the sheets there's a mattress
the old rough kind, with buttons and ticking

under the mattress is a frame
of rusting iron   still strong

the whole bed smells of soap and rust
the window smells of old tobacco-dust and rain

this is your room
in Calle Visión

if you took the turn-off
it was for you

2

Calle Visión   sand in your teeth
granules of cartilage in your wrists

Calle Visión   firestorm behind
shuttered eyelids   fire in your foot

Calle Visión   rocking the gates
of your locked bones

Calle Visión   dreamnet dropped
over your porous sleep

3

Lodged in the difficult hotel
all help withheld

a place not to live but to die in
not an inn but a hospital

a friend's love came to me
touched and took me away

in a car   love
of a curmudgeon, a short-fuse

and as he drove   eyes on the road
I felt his love

and that was simply the case   the way things were
unstated and apparent

and like the rest of it
clear as a dream

4

Calle Visión   your heart beats on unbroken
  how is this possible

Calle Visión   wounded knee
  wounded spine   wounded eye

  Have you ever worked around metal?
  Are there particles under your skin?

Calle Visión   but your heart is still whole
  how is this possible

since what can be   will be taken
  when not offered in trust and faith

by the collectors of collectibles
  the professors of what-has-been-suffered

    The world is falling down   hold my hand
    It's a lonely sound   hold my hand

Calle Visión   never forget
  the body's pain

never divide it

5

Ammonia
       carbon dioxide
            carbon monoxide
                    methane
                hydrogen sulfide
: the gasses that rise from urine and feces

in the pig confinement units known as nurseries
can eat a metal doorknob off in half a year

pig-dander
        dust from dry manure
—lung-scar: breath-shortedness an early symptom

And the fire shall try
every man's work   :Calle Visión:
and every woman's

if you took the turn-off
this is your revelation   this the source

6

The repetitive motions of slaughtering
　　—fire in wrists　in elbows—
the dead birds coming at you along the line
　　—how you smell them in your sleep—
fire in your wrist　blood packed
　　under your fingernails　heavy air
doors padlocked on the outside
　　—you might steal a chicken—
fire in the chicken factory fire
　　in the carpal tunnel　leaping the frying vats
yellow smoke from soybean oil
　　and wasted parts and insulating wire
—some fleeing to the freezer some
　　found "stuck in poses of escape"—

7

You can call on beauty still and it will leap
from all directions

you can write beauty into the cruel file
of things done   things left undone   but

once we were dissimilar
yet unseparate   that's beauty   that's what you catch

in the newborn's midnight gaze
the fog that melts the falling stars

the virus from the smashed lianas driven
searching now for us

8

In the room   in the house
in Calle Visión

all you want   is to lie down
alone on your back   let your hands

slide lightly over your hipbones
But she's there with her remnants her cross-sections

trying to distract you
with her childhood her recipes her

cargo of charred pages her
carved and freckled neck-stones

her crying-out-for-witness her
backward-forward timescapes

her suitcase in Berlin
and the one lost and found

in her island go-and-come
—is she terrified you will forget her?

9

In the black net
of her orange wing

the angry nightblown butterfly
hangs on a piece of lilac in the sun

carried overland like her
from a long way off

She has travelled hard and far
and her interrogation goes:

—*Hands dripping with wet earth*
head full of shocking dreams

O what have you buried all these years
what have you dug up?

This place is alive with the dead and with the living
I have never been alone here

I wear my triple eye as I walk along the road
past, present, future all are at my side

Storm-beaten, tough-winged passenger
there is nothing I have buried that can die

10

On the road there is a house
scrub oak and cactus in the yard

lilac carried overland
from a long way off

in the house there is a bed
on the bed there is a blanket

telling the coming of the railroad
under the mattress there's a frame

of rusting iron   still strong
the window smells of old tobacco-dust and rain

the window smells of old
tobacco-dust and rain

1992–1993

REVERSION

This woman/ the heart of the matter.
This woman flung into solitary by the prayers of her tribe.
This woman waking/ reaching for scissors/ starting to cut
    her hair
Hair long shaven/ growing out.
To snip to snip to snip/ creak of sharpness meeting itself against
    the roughness of her hair.

This woman whose voices drive her into exile.
(Exile, exile.)
Drive her toward the other side.
By train and foot and ship, to the other side.
Other side. Of a narrow sea.

This woman/ the heart of the matter.
Heart of the law/ heart of the prophets.
Their voices buzzing like raspsaws in her brain.
Taking ship without a passport.
How does she do it. Even the ships have eyes.
Are painted like birds.
This woman has no address book.
This woman perhaps has a toothbrush.
Somewhere dealing for red/blue dyes to crest her
    rough-clipped hair.

On the other side: stranger to women and to children.
Setting her bare footsole in the print of the stranger's bare foot in
    the sand.
Feeding the stranger's dog from the sack of her exhaustion.

Hearing the male prayers of the stranger's tribe/   rustle of the
      stranger's river.
Lying down asleep and dreamless in one of their doorways.

She has long shed the coverings.
On the other side she walks bare-armed, bare-legged, clothed
      in voices.
Here or there picks up a scarf/   a remnant.
Day breaks cold on her legs and in her sexual hair.
Her punk hair/   her religious hair.

Passing the blue rectangles of the stranger's doors.
Not one opens to her.
Threading herself into declining alleys/   black on white plaster/
      olive on violet.
To walk to walk to walk.
To lie on a warm stone listening to familiar insects.
(Exile, exile.)

This woman/   the heart of the matter.
Circling back to the city where her name crackles behind
      creviced stones.
This woman who left alone and returns alone.
Whose hair again is covered/   whose arms and neck are covered/
      according to the law.
Underneath her skin has darkened/   her footsoles roughened.
Sand from the stranger's doorway sifting from her plastic
            carry-all/   drifting into the sand
                  whirling around in her old quarter.

1993

REVOLUTION IN PERMANENCE
(1953, 1993)

Through a barn window, three-quartered
the profile of Ethel Rosenberg
stares down past a shattered apple-orchard
into speechless firs.
Speechless this evening.   Last night
the whole countryside thrashed in lowgrade fever
under low swollen clouds
the mist advanced and the wind
tore into one thing then another
—you could think *random* but you know
the patterns are there—
a sick time, and the human body
feeling it, a loss of pressure,
an agitation without purpose . . .
Purpose?   Do you believe
all agitation has an outcome
like revolt, like Bread and Freedom?
—or do you hang on to the picture
of the State as a human body
—some people being heads or hearts
and others only hands or guts or legs?
But she—how did she end up here
in this of all places?
What she is seeing I cannot see,
what I see has her shape.
There's an old scythe propped
in an upper window of the barn—
—does it call up marches of peasants?
what is it with you and this barn?

And, no, it's not an old scythe,
it's an old rag, you see how it twitches.
And Ethel Rosenberg? I've worried about her
through the liquid window in that damp place.
I've thought she was coughing, like me,
but her profile stayed still watching
what held her in that position.

1993

THEN OR NOW

Is it necessary for me to write obliquely
about the situation? Is that what
you would have me do?

FOOD PACKAGES: 1947

Powdered milk, chocolate bars, canned fruit, tea,
salamis, aspirin:
Four packages a month to her old professor in Heidelberg
and his Jewish wife:
Europe is trying to revive an intellectual life
and the widow of the great sociologist needs flour.

Europe is trying/to revive/
with the Jews somewhere else.

The young ex-philosopher tries to feed her teachers
all the way from New York, with orders for butter from Denmark,
sending dispatches into the fog
of the European spirit:
*I am no longer German. I am a Jew and the German language
was once my home.*

1993

INNOCENCE: 1945

"The beauty of it was the guilt.
It entered us, quick *schnapps*,
forked tongue of ice.   The guilt
made us feel innocent again.
We had done nothing while some
extreme measures were taken.   We drifted.   In the
Snow Queen's huge ballrom had dreamed
of the whole world and a new pair of skates.
But we had suffered too.
The miracle was: felt
nothing.   Felt we had done
nothing.   Nothing to do.   Felt free.
And we had suffered, too.
It was that freedom we craved,
cold needle in the bloodstream.
Guilt after all was a feeling."

1993

SUNSET, DECEMBER, 1993

Dangerous of course to draw
parallels   Yet more dangerous to write

as if there were a steady course, we and our poems
protected: the individual life, protected

poems, ideas, gliding
in mid-air, innocent

I walked out on the deck and every board
was luminous with cold dew   It could freeze tonight

Each board is different of course but each does gleam
wet, under a complicated sky: mounds of swollen ink

heavy gray unloading up the coast
a rainbow suddenly and casually

unfolding its span
Dangerous not to think

how the earth still was   in places
while the chimneys shuddered with the first dischargements

1993

DEPORTATIONS

It's happened already while we were still
searching for patterns   A turn of the head
toward a long horizontal window overlooking the city
to see people being taken
neighbors, vendors, paramedicals
hurried from their porches, their tomato stalls
their auto-mechanic arguments
and children from schoolyards
There are far more of the takers-away than the taken
at this point anyway

Then: dream-cut: our house:
four men walk through the unlatched door
One in light summer wool and silken tie
One in work clothes browned with blood
One with open shirt, a thin
thong necklace hasped with silver around his neck
One in shorts naked up from the navel

And they have come for us, two of us and four of them
and I think, perhaps they are still human
and I ask them   *When do you think this all began?*

as if trying to distract them from their purpose
as if trying to appeal to a common bond
as if one of them might be you
as if I were practicing for something
yet to come

1994

AND NOW

And now as you read these poems
—you whose eyes and hands I love
—you whose mouth and eyes I love
—you whose words and minds I love—
don't think I was trying to state a case
or construct a scenery:
I tried to listen to
the public voice of our time
tried to survey our public space
as best I could
—tried to remember and stay
faithful to details, note
precisely how the air moved
and where the clock's hands stood
and who was in charge of definitions
and who stood by receiving them
when the name of compassion
was changed to the name of guilt
when to feel with a human stranger
was declared obsolete.

1994

SENDING LOVE

Voice
from the grain

of the forest bought
and condemned

sketched bond
in the rockmass

the earthquake sought
and threw

Sending love: Molly sends it
Ivan sends it, Kaori

sends it to Brian, Irina sends it
on pale green aerograms Abena sends it

to Charlie and to Joséphine
Arturo sends it, Naomi sends it

Lourdes sends it to Naoual
Walter sends it to Arlene

Habib sends it, Vashti
floats it to Eqbal in a paper plane

Bored in the meeting, on a postcard
Yoel scribbles it to Gerhard

Reza on his e-mail
finds it waiting from Patricia

Mario and Elsie
send it to Francísco

Karolina sends it monthly
home with a money order

June seals it with a kiss to Dahlia
Mai sends it, Montserrat

scrawls it to Faíz on a memo
Lenny wires it with roses

to Lew who takes it on his
whispery breath, Julia sends it

loud and clear, Dagmar brailles it
to Maureen, María Christina

sends it, Meena and Moshe send it
Patrick and Max are always

sending it back and forth
and even Shirley, even George

are found late after closing
sending it, sending it

Sending love is harmless
doesn't bind you   can't make you sick

sending love's expected
precipitous   and wary

sending love can be carefree
Joaquín knew it, Eira knows it

sending love without heart
—well, people do that daily

Terrence years ago
closed the window, wordless

Grace who always laughed is leaning
her cheek against bullet-proof glass

her tears enlarged
like scars on a planet

Vivian hangs her raincoat
on a hook, turns to the classroom

her love entirely
there, supreme

Victor fixes his lens
on disappearing faces

—caught now or who will ever
see them again?

1992—1994

TAKE

At the head of this poem I have laid out
a boning knife a paring knife a wooden spoon a pair of tongs.
Oaken grain beneath them olive and rusty light
around them.
And you looming: This is not your scene
this is the first frame of a film
I have in mind to make: move on, get out.
And you here telling me: What will be done
with these four objects will be done
through my lens not your words.

The poet shrugs: I was only in the kitchen
looking at the chopping board.   (Not the whole story.)
And you telling me: Awful is the scope
of what I have in mind, awful the music I shall deploy, most
awful the witness of the camera moving
out from the chopping board to the grains of snow
whirling against the windowglass to the rotating
searchlights of the tower.   The humped snow-shrouded tanks
laboring toward the border.   This is not your bookish art.

But say the poet picks up the boning knife and thinks *my bones*
if she touching the paring knife thinks *carrot, onion, celery*
if staring at the wooden spoon I see the wood is split
as if from five winters of war
when neither celery, onion, carrot could be found
or picking up the tongs I whisper *What this was for*

And did you say *get on, get out* or just *look out?*
Were you speaking from exhaustion from disaster from your last
        assignment were you afraid

for the vision in the kitchen, that it could not be saved
—no time to unload the heavy
cases to adjust
the sensitive equipment
to seize the olive rusty light to scan the hand that reaches
        hovering
over a boning knife a paring knife a wooden spoon a pair
        of tongs
to cull the snow before it blows away across the border's blacked-
        out sheds
and the moon swims in a bluish bubble dimmed
by the rotating searchlights of the tower?   Here
it is in my shorthand, do what you have in mind.

1994

LATE GHAZAL

Footsole to scalp alive facing the window's black mirror.
First rains of the winter   morning's smallest hour.

Go back to the ghazal then   what will you do there?
Life always pulsed harder than the lines.

Do you remember the strands that ran from eye to eye?
The tongue that reached everywhere, speaking all the parts?

Everything there was cast in an image of desire.
The imagination's cry is a sexual cry.

I took my body anyplace with me.
In the thickets of abstraction my skin ran with blood.

Life was always stronger . . . the critics couldn't get it.
Memory says the music always ran ahead of the words.

1994

SIX NARRATIVES

1

You drew up the story of your life   I was in that story
Nights on the coast I'd meet you flashlight in hand
curving my soles over musseled rocks   cracked and raw we'd lick
        inside the shells for danger
You'd drop into the bar   I'd sit upstairs at my desk writing
        the pages
you hoped would make us famous   then in the face of my
        turned back
you went to teach at the freedom school as if
you were teaching someone else to get free from me   this was
        your story
Like a fogsmeared planet over the coast
I'd walked into, served, your purposeful longings   I knew, I did
        not stop   till I turned my back

2

You drew up a story about me   I fled that story
Aching in mind I noticed names on the helms of busses:
        COP CITY   SHEEPSHEAD BAY
I thought I saw the city where the cops came home
to lay kitchen linoleum   barbecue on balconies
I saw the bloodied head of the great sheep dragged through
        the underpasses
trucked to the bay where the waters would not touch it
left on the beach in its shroud of flies
On the bus to La Guardia my arms ached with all my findings
anchored under my breasts with all my will
I cried *sick day, O sick day, this is my day and I, for this I will*
        not pay
as the green rushed bleeding out through the snarled cracks of
        the expressway

3

You were telling a story about women to young men   It was
        not my story
it was not a story about women it was a story about men
Your hunger a spear gripped in hand a tale unspun in your
        rented campground
clothed in captured whale-songs tracked with synthesized
        Andes flutes
it was all about you   beaded and bearded   misfeathered and
        miscloaked
where the TV cameras found you in your sadness

4

You were telling a story about love   it was your story
I came and stood outside
listening :   : death was in the doorway
death was in the air but the story
had its own life   no pretenses
about women in that lovesong for a man
Listening I went inside the bow scraping the bass-string
inside the horn's heartbroken cry
I was the breath's intake the bow's rough mutter:
Vigil for boy of responding kisses, (never again on earth responding,)
Vigil for comrade swiftly slain . . .

5

I was telling you a story about love
how even in war it goes on speaking its own language

Yes you said but the larynx is bloodied
the knife was well-aimed into the throat

Well I said love is hated   it has no price

No you said   you are talking about feelings
Have you ever felt nothing?   that is what war is now

Then a shadow skimmed your face
Go on talking in a normal voice   you murmured
Nothing is listening

6

You were telling a story about war   it is our story
an old story   and still it must be told
the story of the new that fled the old
how the big dream strained and shifted
the ship of hope shuddered on the iceberg's breast
the private affections swayed and staggered
So we are thrown together   so we are racked apart
in a republic shivering on   its glassy lips
parted   as if the fundamental rift
had not been calculated from the first into the mighty scaffold.

1994

FROM PIERCÉD DARKNESS

New York/December

Taking the least griefcrusted avenue the last worst bridge away
somewhere beyond her Lost & Found we stopped in our flight to
   check backward
in the rearview mirror into her piercéd darkness.   A mirror is
   either flat or deep
and ours was deep to the vanishing point: we saw showroom
   mannequins draped and trundled
—black lace across blackening ice—
false pearls knotted by nervous fingers, backribs lacquered in
   sauce.
Narrow waters rocking in spasms.   The torch hand-held and the
   poem of entrance.
Topless towers turned red and green.
Dripping faucet icicled radiator.
Eyes turned inward.   Births arced into dumpsters.
Eyes blazing under knitted caps,
hands gripped on taxi-wheels, steering.
Fir bough propped in a cardboard doorway, bitter tinsel.
The House of the Jewish Book, the Chinese Dumpling House.
Swaddled limbs dreaming on stacked shelves of sleep   opening
   like knives.

Her piercéd darkness.   Dragqueen dressed to kill in beauty
drawing her bridgelit shawls
over her shoulders.   Her caves ghosted by foxes.   Her tracked
   arms.
Who climbs the subway stairs at the end of night

---

lugging a throwaway banquet.   Her
Man Who Lived Underground and all his children.
Nightcrews uncapping her streets wildlamps strung up on high.

————————

Fairy lights charming stunted trees.
Hurt eyes awake to the glamor.
I've walked this zone
gripping my nightstick, worked these rooms
in silver silk charmeuse and laid my offerings
next to the sexless swathed form lying in the doorway.
I've preached for justice rubbing crumbs
from sticky fingers for the birds.
Picked up a pretty chain of baubles
in the drugstore, bitten them to see if they were real.
I've boiled a stocking and called it Christmas pudding.
Bought freeborn eggs to cook
with sugar, milk and pears.

————————

Altogether the angels arrive for the chorus
in rapidly grabbed robes they snatch scores of hallelujahs
complicit with television cameras they bend down their eyes.
However they sing their voices will glisten
in the soundmix.   All of it good enough for us.
Altogether children will wake before the end of night
("not good dawn" my Jewish grandmother called it) will stand
            as we did
handheld in cold dark before the parents' door
singing for glimpsed gilt and green
packages, the drama, the power of the hour.

————————

Black lace, blackening ice. To give on one designated day—
a window bangs shut on an entire
forcefield of chances, connections.   A window flies open
on the churning of birds in flight going surely somewhere else.
A snowflake like no other flies past, we will not hear of it
again, we will surely
hear of it
again.

1994–1995

INSCRIPTIONS

ONE: COMRADE

Little as I knew you I know you: little as you knew me you
          know me
—that's the light we stand under when we meet.
I've looked into flecked jaws
walked injured beaches footslick in oil
watching licked birds stumble in flight
while you drawn through the pupil of your eye
across your own oceans in visionary pain and in relief
headlong and by choice took on the work of charting
your city's wounds ancient and fertile
listening for voices within and against.
My testimony: yours: Trying to keep faith
not with each other exactly yet it's the one known and unknown
who stands for, imagines the other   with whom faith could
          be kept.

In city your mind burns wanes waxes with hope
(no stranger to bleakness you: worms have toothed at
          your truths
but you were honest regarding that).
You conspired to compile the illegal discography
of songs forbidden to sing or to be heard.
If there were ethical flowers one would surely be yours
and I'd hand it to you headlong across landmines
across city's whyless sleeplight I'd hand it
purposefully, with love, a hand trying to keep beauty afloat
on the bacterial waters.

When a voice learns to sing it can be heard as dangerous
when a voice learns to listen it can be heard as desperate.

The self unlocked to many selves.
A mirror handed to one who just released
from the locked ward from solitary from preventive detention
sees in her thicket of hair her lost eyebrows
whole populations.
One who discharged from war stares in the looking-glass of home
at what he finds there, sees in the undischarged tumult of his
　　　　own eye
how thickskinned peace is, and those who claim to promote it.

TWO: MOVEMENT

Old backswitching road bent toward the ocean's light
Talking of angles of vision   movements   a black or a red tulip
        opening
Times of walking across a street   thinking
not *I have joined a movement* but   *I am stepping in this deep current*
Part of my life washing behind me   terror I couldn't swim with
part of my life waiting for me   a part I had no words for
I need to live each day through   have them and know them all
though I can see from here where I'll be standing at the end.

———————

When does a life bend toward freedom?   grasp its direction?
How do you know you're not circling in pale dreams, nostalgia,
        stagnation
but entering that deep current   malachite, colorado
requiring all your strength wherever found
your patience and your labor
desire pitted against desire's inversion
all your mind's fortitude?
Maybe through a teacher: someone with facts with numbers
        with poetry
who wrote on the board: IN EVERY GENERATION ACTION FREES
        OUR DREAMS.
Maybe a student: one mind unfurling like a redblack peony
quenched into percentile, dropout, stubbed-out bud
—Your journals Patricia: Douglas your poems: but the repeti-
        tive blows
on spines whose hope you were, on yours:
to see that quenching and decide.

—And now she turns her face brightly on the new morning in
       the new classroom
new in her beauty her skin her lashes her lively body:
Race, class . . . all that . . . but isn't all that just history?
Aren't people bored with it all?

She could be
myself at nineteen   but free of reverence for past ideas
ignorant of hopes piled on her   She's a mermaid
momentarily precipitated from a solution
which could stop her heart   She could swim or sink
like a beautiful crystal.

THREE: ORIGINS

Turning points.   We all like to hear about those.   Points
        on a graph.
Sudden conversions.   Historical swings.   Some kind of
        dramatic structure.
But a life doesn't unfold that way   it moves
in loops   by switchbacks loosely strung
around the swelling of one hillside toward another
one island toward another
A child's knowing   a child's forgetting   remain childish
till you meet them   mirrored and echoing   somewhere else
Don't ask me when I learned love
Don't ask me when I learned fear
Ask about the size of rooms   how many lived in them
        what else the rooms contained
        what whispers of the histories of skin

Should I simplify my life for you?
The Confederate Women of Maryland
on their dried-blood granite pedestal incised
                IN DIFFICULTY AND IN DANGER . . .
                    "BRAVE AT HOME"
—words a child could spell out
standing in wetgreen grass stuck full of yellow leaves
monumental women bandaging wounded men
Joan of Arc in a book   a peasant in armor
Mussolini   Amelia Earhart   the President on the radio
        —what's taught, what's overheard

Should I simplify my life for you?
Don't ask how I began to love men.
Don't ask how I began to love women.
Remember the forties songs, the slowdance numbers
the small sex-filled gas-rationed Chevrolet?
Remember walking in the snow and who was gay?
Cigarette smoke of the movies, silver-and-gray
profiles, dreaming the dreams of he-and-she
breathing the dissolution of the wisping silver plume?
Dreaming that dream we leaned applying lipstick
by the gravestone's mirror when we found ourselves
playing in the cemetery.   In Current Events she said
the war in Europe is over, the Allies
and she wore no lipstick have won the war
and we raced screaming out of Sixth Period.

Dreaming that dream
we had to maze our ways through a wood
where lips were knives breasts razors and I hid
in the cage of my mind scribbling
this map stops where it all begins
into a red-and-black notebook.
Remember after the war when peace came down
as plenty for some and they said we were saved
in an eternal present and we knew the world could end?
—remember after the war when peace rained down
on the winds from Hiroshima Nagasaki Utah Nevada?
and the socialist queer Christian teacher jumps from the
              hotel window?
and L.G. saying *I want to sleep with you but not for sex*

and the red-and-black enamelled coffee-pot dripped slow through
        the dark grounds
—appetite terror power tenderness
the long kiss in the stairwell the switch thrown
on two Jewish Communists married to each other
the definitive crunch of glass at the end of the wedding?
(When shall we learn, what should be clear as day,
We cannot choose what we are free to love?)

"That year I began to understand the words *burden of proof*
—how the free market of ideas depended
on certain lives laboring under that burden.
I started feeling in my body
how that burden was bound to our backs
keeping us cramped in old repetitive motions
crouched in the same mineshaft year on year
or like children in school striving to prove
proofs already proven over and over
to get into the next grade
but there is no next grade no movement onward only this

and the talk goes on, the laws, the jokes, the deaths, the way of
        life goes on
as if you had proven nothing as if this burden were what
        you are."

_____

(Knotted crowns of asparagus lowered by human hands
into long silver trenches fogblanched mornings
the human spine translated into fog's
almost unbearable rheumatic beauty flattering pain
into a daze a mystic text of white and white's
absolute faceless romance : : the photographer's
darkroom thrill discerning two phantoms caught
trenchside deep in the delicate power
of fog : : phantoms who nonetheless have to know
the length of the silvery trenches how many plants how long
this bending can go on and for what wage and what
that wage will buy in the Great Central Valley 1983.)

———————

"Desire disconnected   meetings and marches
for justice and peace   the sex of the woman
the bleached green-and-gold   of the cotton print bedspread
in the distance the sound   of the week's demonstration
July sun louvered shutters   off Riverside Drive
shattered glass in the courtyard   the sex of the woman
her body entire aroused to the hair
the sex of the women our bodies entire
molten in purpose each body a tongue
each body a river and over and over

and after to walk   in the streets still unchanging
a stormy light, evening   tattered emblems, horse-droppings
DO NOT CROSS POLICE BARRIER   yellow boards kicked awry
the scattering crowds   at the mouth of the subway

A thumbprint on a glass of icy water
memory that scours and fogs

nights when I threw my face
on a sheet of lithic scatter
wrapped myself in a sack of tears"

———————

"My thief   my counsellor
        tell me how it was then under the bridge
        in the long cashmere scarf
        the opera-lover left
silken length rough flesh violet light meandering
the splash that trickled down the wall
O tell me what you hissed to him and how he groaned to you
tell me the opera-lover's body limb by limb and touch by touch

———————

how his long arms arched dazzling under the abutment
     as he played himself to the hilt
     cloak flocked with light
My thief   my counsellor
tell me was it good or bad, was it good and bad, in the
     unbefriended archway of your first ardor?
was it an oilstain's thumbprint on moving water?
the final drench and fizzle on the wall?
was it freedom from names from rank from color?
Thieving the leather trenchcoat of the night, my counsellor?
Breathing the sex of night of water never having to guess its
     source, my thief?

O thief
I stand at your bedside   feed you segments of orange
O counsellor
you have too many vanishing children to attend
There were things I was meant to learn from you   they wail out
     like a train leaving the city
Desire the locomotive   death the tracks   under the bridge
the silken roughness drench of freedom the abruptly
     floodlit parapet
LOVE CONQUERS ALL spelled out in flickering graffiti
—my counsellor, my thief"

_____

"In the heart of the capital of Capital
against banked radiations of azalea
I found a faux-marble sarcophagus inscribed
               HERE LIES THE WILL OF THE PEOPLE
I had been wondering why for so long so little
had been heard from that quarter.
I found myself there by deepest accident
wandering among white monuments
looking for the Museum of Lost Causes.

_____

A strangely focused many-lumened glare
was swallowing alive the noon.
I saw the reviewing stand the podium draped and swagged
the huge screen all-enhancing and all-heightening
I heard the martial bands the choirs the speeches
amplified in the vacant plaza
swearing to the satellites it had been a natural death."

SIX: EDGELIT

Living under fire in the raincolored opal of your love
I could have forgotten other women I desired
so much I wanted to love them but
here are some reasons love would not let me:
One had a trick of dropping her lashes along her cheekbone
in an amazing screen so she saw nothing.
Another would stand in summer arms rounded and warm
catching wild apricots that fell
either side of a broken fence but she caught them on one
            side only.
One, ambitious, flushed
to the collarbone, a shapely coward.
One keen as mica, glittering,
full at the lips, absent at the core.
One who flirted with danger
had her escape route planned when others had none
and disappeared.
One sleepwalking on the trestle
of privilege dreaming of innocence
tossing her cigarette into the dry gully
—an innocent gesture.

                    _____

Medbh's postcard from Belfast:
                    one's poetry seems aimless
covered in the blood and lies
                    oozing corrupt & artificial
but of course one will continue . . .

This week I've dredged my pages

                                                    _____

for anything usable
                head, heart, perforated
by raw disgust and fear
If I dredge up anything it's suffused
by what it works in, "like the dyer's hand"
I name it unsteady, slick, unworthy
                and I go on

In my sixty-fifth year I know something about language:
it can eat or be eaten by experience
Medbh, poetry means refusing
the choice to kill or die

but this life of continuing is for the sane mad
and the bravest monsters

————————

The bright planet that plies her crescent shape
in the western air   that through the screendoor gazes
with her curved eye now speaks: *The beauty of darkness
is how it lets you see.*   Through the screendoor
she told me this and half-awake I scrawled
her words on a piece of paper.
She is called Venus but I call her You
You   who sees me   You   who calls me to see
You   who has other errands far away in space and time
You   in your fiery skin   acetylene
scorching the claims of the false mystics
You   who like the moon arrives in crescent
changeable changer   speaking truth from darkness

————————

Edgelit: firegreen yucca under fire-ribbed clouds
blue-green agave   grown huge in flower
cries of birds streaming over

The night of the eclipse the full
moon
swims clear between flying clouds until

the hour of the occlusion   It's not of aging
anymore and its desire
which is of course unending

it's of dying   young or old
in full desire

Remember me . . . . O, O, O,
O, remember me

these vivid stricken cells
precarious living marrow
this my labyrinthine filmic brain
this my dreaded blood
this my irreplaceable
footprint vanishing from the air

dying in full desire
thirsting for the coldest water
hungering for hottest food
gazing into the wildest light

edgelight from the high desert
where shadows drip from tiniest stones
sunlight of bloody afterglow

torque of the Joshua tree
flinging itself forth in winter
factoring freeze into its liquid consciousness

These are the extremes I stoke
into the updraft of this life
still roaring

                    into thinnest air

1993–1994

NOTES

WHAT KIND OF TIMES ARE THESE

Page 1: The title is from Bertolt Brecht's poem "An Die Nachge-
borenen" ("For Those Born Later"): *What kind of times are these /
When it's almost a crime to talk about trees / Because it means keeping
still about so many evil deeds?* (For the complete poem, in a different
translation, see John Willett and Ralph Manheim, eds., *Bertolt
Brecht, Poems 1913–1956* [New York: Methuen, 1976], pp. 318–
320.)

Page 3: "our country moving closer to its own truth and dread
. . ." echoes Osip Mandelstam's 1921 poem that begins *I was
washing outside in the darkness* and ends *The earth's moving closer to
truth and to dread.* (Clarence Brown and W. S. Merwin, trans.,
Osip Mandelstam: Selected Poems [New York: Atheneum, 1974], p.
40.) Mandelstam was forbidden to publish, then exiled and sen-
tenced to five years of hard labor for a poem caricaturing Stalin;
he died in a transit camp in 1938.

Page 5: "To be human, said Rosa . . . ." Rosa Luxemburg (1871–
1919) was a Polish-born middle-class Jew. Early in her abbre-
viated life she entered the currents of European socialist revolu-
tionary thinking and action. She became one of the most
influential and controversial figures in the social-democratic move-
ments of Eastern Europe and Germany. Besides her political es-
says, she left hundreds of vivid letters to friends and comrades.
Imprisoned during World War I for her strongly internationalist
and anticapitalist beliefs, she was murdered in Berlin in 1919 by
right-wing soldiers, with the passive collusion of a faction from
her own party. Her body was thrown into a canal.

On December 28, 1916, from prison, she wrote a New Year
letter to friends she feared were both backsliding and complaining:
"Then see to it that you remain a *Mensch!* [Yiddish/German for
human being] . . . Being a *Mensch* means happily throwing one's

life 'on fate's great scale' if necessary, but, at the same time, enjoying every bright day and every beautiful cloud. Oh, I can't write you a prescription for being a *Mensch*. I only know how one is a *Mensch*, and you used to know it too when we went walking for a few hours in the Südende fields with the sunset's red light falling on the wheat. The world is so beautiful even with all its horrors." (*The Letters of Rosa Luxemburg*, ed., trans. and with an intro. by Stephen Eric Bronner [Atlantic Highlands, N.J.: Humanities Press, 1993], p. 173.)

CALLE VISIÓN

Page 9: Calle Visión is the name of a road in the southwestern United States—literally, "Vision Street."

Page 11: "that tells the coming of the railroad." "With the coming of the railroad, new materials and pictorial designs and motifs, including trains themselves, appeared in Navaho weaving (ca. 1880)." (From the Museum of Indian Arts and Culture, Museum of New Mexico, Santa Fe.)

Page 13: "a place not to live but to die in." See Sir Thomas Browne, *Religio Medici* (1635): "For the World, I count it not an Inn, but an Hospital; and a place not to live, but to dye in." (*Religio Medici and Other Writings by Sir Thomas Browne* [London: Everyman's Library, J. M. Dent, 1947], p. 83.)

Page 14: "Have you ever worked around metal? . . . ." From a questionnaire filled out before undergoing a magnetic resonance imaging (MRI) scan.

Page 14: "The world is falling down . . . ." From the song "The World Is Falling Down," composed by Abbey Lincoln, sung by her on the Verve recording of the same title, 1990 (Moseka Music BMI).

Page 15: "And the fire shall try . . . ." 1 Corinthians 3:13: "Every man's work shall be made manifest . . . and the fire shall try every man's work of what sort it is." Used by Studs Terkel as an epigraph to his *Working* (New York: Pantheon, 1974).

REVERSION

Page 21: This poem is for Nina Menkes and her film *The Great Sadness of Zohara.*

REVOLUTION IN PERMANENCE (1953, 1993)

Page 23: The phrase "revolution in permanence" is Marx's, referring to his concept that the creation of a just society does not end with the uprooting of the old order, "but must continue to the new, so you begin to feel this presence of the future in the present." (Raya Dunayevskaya, *Marxism and Freedom* [New York: Columbia University Press, 1988], p. 12.)

In the poem, Ethel Rosenberg is a secular vision. But she was, of course, a real woman, electrocuted in 1953 with her husband, Julius, on charges of conspiracy to commit espionage. The original charges were rapidly translated by the presiding judge and the media into "selling the secret of the atomic bomb" to agents of the Soviet Union. After the Rosenbergs' conviction, "twenty-three motions and appeals for new trial, reduction of sentence, stay of execution, and presidential clemency were made on the basis of perjury; unfair trial; cruel, excessive, inapplicable, and unprecedented sentencing; newly discovered evidence; suborna-tion of perjury by the prosecution; application of incorrect law; and justice, mercy, or both. All appeals were denied. . . . [The day after the electrocution] Justice Hugo Black's majority opinion was published, noting that the Supreme Court 'had never reviewed the record of this trial and therefore never affirmed the fairness of this trial.' " (Virginia Carmichael, *Framing History: The Rosen-berg Story and the Cold War* [Minneapolis: University of Minnesota Press, 1993], pp. 63–64. See also Walter and Miriam Schneir, *Invitation to an Inquest* [New York: Pantheon, 1983]; Robert and Michael Meeropol, *We Are Your Sons: The Legacy of Ethel and Julius Rosenberg* [Urbana and Chicago: University of Illinois Press, 1986]; and Michael Meeropol, ed., *The Rosenberg Letters: A Complete Edition of the Prison Correspondence of Julius and Ethel Rosenberg* [New York: Garland, 1994].

THEN OR NOW

Page 25: This sequence of poems derives in part from Hannah Arendt and Karl Jaspers, *Correspondence 1926–1969*, ed. Lotte and Hans Saner, trans. Robert and Rita Kimbel (New York: Harcourt Brace Jovanovich, 1992). While reading these letters, I had been reflecting on concepts of "guilt" and "innocence" among artists and intellectuals like myself in the United States. The poems owe much also to the continuing pressure of events.

LATE GHAZAL

Page 43: See "Ghazals (Homage to Ghalib)" and "The Blue Ghazals," in Adrienne Rich, *Collected Early Poems: 1950–1970* (New York: Norton, 1993), pp. 339–355, 368–372. See also Aijaz Ahmad, ed., *Ghazals of Ghalib* (New York: Columbia University Press, 1971).

SIX NARRATIVES

Page 45: The narratives are spoken by different voices.

Page 50: "Vigil for boy of responding kisses, . . ." See Walt Whitman, "Vigil strange I kept on the field one night," in *The Essential Whitman*, selected and ed. Galway Kinnell (New York: Ecco Press, 1987), pp. 123–124.

INSCRIPTIONS

Page 61: "I need to live each day through . . . ." These two lines are quoted from an earlier poem of mine ("8/8/68: I") in "Ghazals (Homage to Ghalib)"; see above.

Page 65: "When shall we learn, what should be clear as day, . . . ?" These two lines are from W. H. Auden's "Canzone," in *The Collected Poetry of W. H. Auden* (New York: Random House, 1945), p. 161.

Page 70: "Medbh's postcard from Belfast." I thank the Northern Irish poet Medbh McGuckian for permission to quote her words from a postcard received in August 1994.

Page 71: "suffused / by what it works in, 'like the dyer's hand.' "

I had written "suffused," later began looking up the line I was quoting from memory: was it Coleridge? Keats? Shakespeare? My friend Barbara Gelpi confirmed it was Shakespeare, in his Sonnet 111: *Thence comes it that my name receives a brand / And almost thence my nature is subdued / To what it works in, like the dyer's hand.* I have kept "suffused" here because to feel *suffused* by the materials that one has perforce to work in is not necessarily to be *subdued,* though some might think so.